DIWALI—
HINDU FESTIVAL
OF LIGHTS

REVISED AND UPDATED

Dianne M. MacMillan

Enslow Elementary

an imprint of

Enslow Publishers, Inc.

40 Industrial Road
Box 398
Berkeley Heights, NJ 07922
USA

http://www.enslow.com

To Padmini and Prashant

Acknowledgments

The author wishes to thank Sreemala S. Setty for generously sharing her beautiful culture. Thanks also go to Thomas Myladil, professor of Hinduism at Rutgers University, for his careful review of the manuscript, and to Michael Witzel, professor of Indic languages at Harvard University, for his review of the Hindi language and pronunciations used in this book

Enslow Elementary, an imprint of Enslow Publishers, Inc.

Enslow Elementary® is a registered trademark of Enslow Publishers, Inc.

Copyright © 2008 by Enslow Publishers, Inc.

All rights reserved.

No part of this book may be reproduced by any means without the written permission of the publisher.

Library of Congress Cataloging-in-Publication Data

MacMillan, Dianne M., 1943–
　　Diwali : Hindu festival of lights / Dianne M. MacMillan. — [Rev. and updated ed.].
　　　　p. cm. — (Best holiday books)
　　Previously published: Springfield, NJ : Enslow Publishers, c1997.
　　Summary: "Read about the history of Diwali and see how it is celebrated in the United States"—Provided by publisher.
　　Includes bibliographical references and index.
　　ISBN-13: 978-0-7660-3060-2
　　ISBN-10: 0-7660-3060-1
　　1. Divali—Juvenile literature. I. Title.
　　BL1239.82.D58M23　2008
　　294.5'36—dc22

　　　　　　　　　　　　　　　　　　　　　　　　　2007002420

Printed in the United States of America

10 9 8 7 6 5 4 3 2 1

To Our Readers: We have done our best to make sure all Internet Addresses in this book were active and appropriate when we went to press. However, the author and the publisher have no control over and assume no liability for the material available on those Internet sites or on other Web sites they may link to. Any comments or suggestions can be sent by e-mail to comments@enslow.com or to the address on the back cover.

Illustration Credits: Associated Press, pp. 1, 4, 6, 8, 14, 16, 26, 28, 36 (top right), 41, 42; © ArkReligion.com/Alamy, p. 32; Artvale, p. 10; Corel, pp. 19, 23, 27; Courtesy Ian and Wendy Sewell, ianandwendy.com, p. 12; © 2007 Jupiterimages Corporation, p. 22; © 2005 Hindu Students Council at MIT, 37; © istockphoto.com/Peter Miller, p. 38 (top left); Shutterstock, pp. 3, 7 13, 30, 31, 34, 36 (bottom), 38 (bottom right), 40, 43.

Cover Photo: Associated Press

Contents

A woman lights a dipa as children play with sparklers in New Delhi, India.

HUNDREDS OF LIGHTS

As the sun goes down, in many homes in the United States and Canada, mothers light tiny clay oil lamps outside their homes. These tiny oil lamps are called dipa (DEE-pah). Children follow behind their mother. As each new point of light glows brightly on the walls and window ledges, the children smile. Soon rows of lights are seen everywhere.

These children each get ready to paint their own dipa for Diwali.

Every light in the house is turned on. The darkness of the night is pushed away. Good feelings fill the night air.

After eating a delicious meal, everyone goes outside. If the family lives in a city that allows fireworks, small firecrackers and sparklers are set off amid shouts of laughter. Even if fireworks are not

A dipa is a small oil lamp made from clay. These lamps are an important part of Diwali.

Indian children paint their faces for a 2002 Diwali fair in Bombay, India.

allowed, the family can still admire the dozens of burning lights.

These Indian-American families are celebrating a Hindu holiday that began thousands of years ago in the country of India. Hindus are members of one of the world's largest religions. The holiday is called Diwali (di-WAH-lee).

Diwali takes place in the month of October or November. It is one of the most joyous holidays of the year. It is also called Festival of Lights. Festival is another word for holiday or celebration. Let's find out more about this special day.

> Diwali, the Festival of Lights, is one of the most joyous holidays of the year.

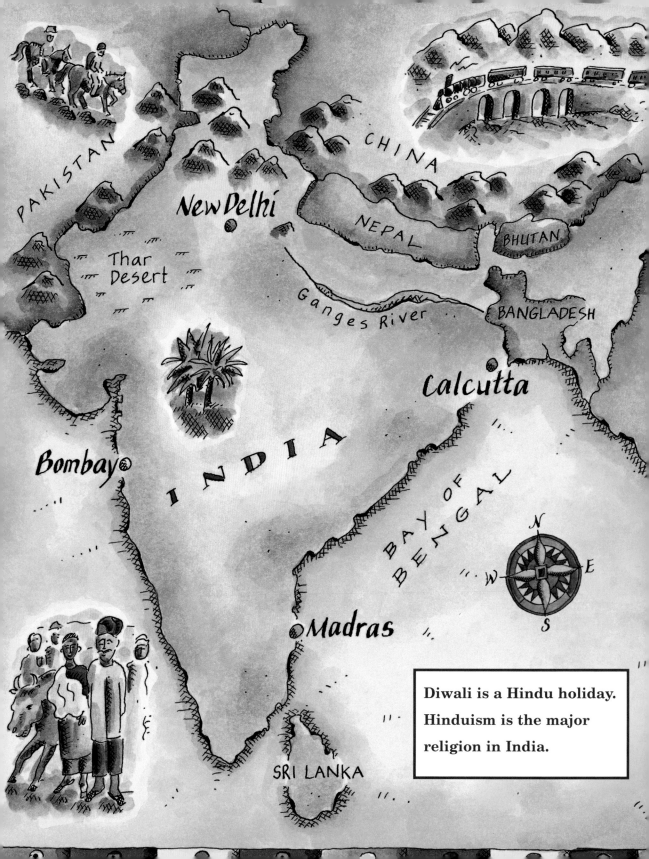

PAKISTAN

CHINA

New Delhi

Thar Desert

NEPAL

BHUTAN

Ganges River

BANGLADESH

Calcutta

Bombay

INDIA

BAY OF BENGAL

N

W E

S

Madras

SRI LANKA

Diwali is a Hindu holiday. Hinduism is the major religion in India.

HINDUISM

THE MAJOR RELIGION IN INDIA IS HINDUISM. People who follow this religion are called Hindus. Hinduism is one of the oldest of the world's religions. No one knows how the religion started.

Many Indian Americans and Indian Canadians were born in the country of India. If you look on a globe of the world, the country of India is directly opposite the United States on the other side of the world. India is one third the size of the United

States. It is bordered by the countries of Nepal, Afghanistan, Pakistan, China, Bhutan, Burma, Bangladesh, and Sri Lanka.

Sacred writings of Hinduism are contained in four books called the Vedas (VE-das). "Veda" means "knowledge." In the same way that Christians and Jews have the Bible and Muslims have the Qur'an, Hindus read the Vedas. The Vedas contain stories about creation, prayers, and the proper way for a person to live his or her life.

The Golden Temple is located in Punjab, India. It is an important part of celebrating Diwali for many people who live in India.

Hindus believe that when a person dies, his or her soul will be reborn as something or someone else. This rebirth is called "reincarnation." "Karma" means "deeds" or "actions." Hindus believe that good deeds or karma in this life will bring a better birth in the next life. The purpose of each life is to improve oneself until all evil and earthly desires are overcome.

Another belief of Hinduism is that God is in everything: in trees, rivers, and cows. Cows are sacred, so Hindus do not eat beef. The milk from a cow is a symbol of life. A symbol stands for an idea or thing. Milk is used in many Indian foods. It is also used in ceremonies. A ceremony is a set of actions done the same way every time, usually to celebrate a special event.

Cows are sacred to Hindus. This is a sacred cow in Agra, India.

Hindus do not have a holy day in the week as do Christians, Jews, and Muslims.

Some families visit a Hindu temple daily. Others seldom go. Each Hindu worships in his or her own way.

Most families have statues or idols of their favorite gods and goddesses in their homes. Many also have a small altar. The altar is where they pray and worship. They offer food to their gods and goddesses in ceremonies.

A Hindu worship and prayer ceremony is called a puja (POO-jah). A festival for a god or goddess would include a puja in honor of that god. Pujas have special prayers and chants.

Hinduism is a way of life as well as a religion. It suggests right ways for people to live. Hindus believe in one Supreme Being called Brahman (BRAH-mahn). This one Supreme Being has three

A teenage boy in Manassas Park, Virginia, lights candles during a puja.

parts. Brahma (BRAH-mah) is the Creator. Shiva (SHI-vah) is the Destroyer. Vishnu (VISH-noo) is the Preserver. Vishnu has a kindly nature, and Hindus believe that he maintains the universe.

Hindus believe that when the world is in danger, Vishnu takes the form of a human or animal and comes to Earth to save it. The human form of a god is called an avatar (A-vah-tahr).

> Stories and legends about the gods show people how to live their lives the right way.

Many stories have been told about the avatars. Hindus believe that Vishnu has taken the form of an avatar nine times. The two most popular avatars are Rama (RAH-mah) and Krishna (KRISH-nah), the seventh and eighth avatars of Vishnu. Stories and legends about these gods give people an example of how to live their lives the right way. Diwali is a celebration of these examples.

These children in Nasik, India, are dressed up as the god Rama, right, and the goddess Sita.

THE STORY OF RAMA

LONG AGO, A KING WHO RULED IN NORTHERN India had three wives. He also had four sons: Rama, Lakshman (LAK-shman), Bharat (BAH-raht), and Shatrugan (SHAH-tru-gahn).

Rama was brave and handsome and good with a bow and arrow. The people of the kingdom loved him. Rama always tried to do good deeds. He was a good son and brother. When he grew up, he married

Sita (SEE-tah) and became a good husband.

The king wanted to make Rama the next king. One of the king's wives objected. She wanted her son, Bharat, to be the next king. She also asked the king to send Rama away or exile him.

> The King exiled Rama from his kingdom for fourteen years.

Earlier, the king had promised to give this wife two wishes. Even though the king was heartsick, he had to honor his word. He exiled Rama from his kingdom for fourteen years.

Rama quietly obeyed his father. He left with Sita and his brother Lakshman. They wandered in the thick jungles for many years, living off berries, nuts, and small animals that Rama and Lakshman hunted. Often they fought the wild animals and evil spirits, or demons. But Rama always won.

When they got all the way to the southern tip of India, the ten-headed demon king of the island Lanka (Sri Lanka) decided to steal Sita away. He waited until Rama and Lakshman were away hunting. Then he grabbed Sita and flew away to his palace.

Rama was heartbroken. He and his brother searched everywhere for Sita. Then Hanuman (HAH-nu-mahn), a god in the form of a monkey, agreed to help. This god could fly like a bird. Hanuman flew across the ocean and found Sita sitting in the demon king's garden. He dropped Rama's ring into Sita's lap and told her that help was on the way.

All of the animals of the jungle helped Rama and Lakshman build a

This is a painting of Hanuman, the god in monkey form who helped Rama save Sita.

bridge across the ocean to Lanka. Then Rama went across, killed the demon king, and rescued Sita.

> The joyous people lit lamps to guide Rama home.

The fourteen years of exile were over. Rama, Sita, and Lakshman returned home. The night of Rama's return was on the new moon. The joyous people lit lamps to guide him home. This is one of the reasons that Indian people celebrate Diwali as the Festival of Lights.

THE STORY OF KRISHNA

THE STORIES ABOUT KRISHNA, THE EIGHTH avatar of Vishnu, are also some of the best-loved tales of Diwali. He had superhuman strength. When Krishna grew up, he became a great ruler. He took part in a war against the forces of evil.

Krishna's defeat of the evil Narakasura (nah-rah-KAH-su-rah) is always told on Diwali. With his armies, Narakasura captured thousands of maidens and elephants. He rode into villages and stole gold and treasure. One day, he stole the earrings of the mother of the gods. Krishna was asked to help fight against Narakasura.

Krishna, on the horse, is the eighth avatar of Vishnu.

Krishna climbed on his large bird, Garuda (gah-ROO-dah). The Garuda is a mythical creature that is half man and half eagle. Krishna flew to Narakasura's palace. He took his weapons with him: a mace (a heavy metal club), bows and arrows, a gold discus (a round disk), and a conch shell.

He found the palace guarded by mountains, weapons, water, fire, and wind. There was also a fearsome five-headed guard named Mura (MOO-rah).

As they neared the palace, the mountains blocked their way. With a mighty swing of his mace, Krishna shattered the mountains.

Immediately, swords, spears, clubs, and other weapons flew through the air toward him. Using his bow and arrows, Krishna destroyed each weapon before any could reach him.

Next a huge wave of water tried to drown him. Krishna threw his discus at the huge wave. As the discus entered the water, the huge wave turned into gentle rain.

But then the rain was dried by scorching fire as flames surrounded Krishna on all sides. Strong winds fed the fire. Once more, Krishna threw his discus.

A dancer performs the part of Garuda, who helped Krishna defeat the evil Narakasura.

The whirling discus put out the fire and tamed the winds. Finally Krishna reached the palace. He blew into his conch shell.

The noise woke Mura, the five-headed guard. Mura rushed to attack Krishna. Krishna again threw his discus. The edge of the discus cut off all five of Mura's heads. Seeing this, Narakasura was filled with rage. He climbed on his elephant and charged toward Krishna. Narakasura heard a whirring noise. He looked up and saw the discus coming toward him. In the next second, the discus struck. The evil Narakasura was dead.

> Krishna threw his discus, cutting off all five of Mura's heads.

Krishna returned all the treasure, elephants, and young maidens that Narakasura had stolen. He also returned the earrings to the mother of the gods.

Rama and Krishna are both symbols of goodness.

HOW DIWALI BEGAN

THE WORD DIWALI MEANS "ROW OF LIGHTS." No one knows for sure when the first Diwali was celebrated. The holiday is probably as old as the Hindu religion.

Each year, the stories of Rama and Krishna are told again and again. Actors and dancers act out each story. Children

Two girls dance at the Detroit Historical Museum during an East Indian cultural workshop.

love to play the parts of Rama and Krishna. They put on shows for their parents and friends.

Lakshmi (LAHK-shmee), the goddess of good fortune and wealth, has come to symbolize Diwali for most Hindus. They believe Lakshmi blesses homes and

This ballet of the Ramayana was performed at the Prambanan temple in Java.

A woman in Allahabad, India, sells statues of Lakshmi.

businesses on Diwali. People light lamps so Lakshmi can find their homes.

Diwali, the Festival of Lights, celebrates the victory of good deeds over evil ones. The Festival of Lights shines bright for all these reasons.

GETTING READY
FOR DIWALI

INDIANS FOLLOW THE LUNAR CALENDAR. Each month begins with the new moon and lasts until the next new moon. The month is twenty-nine and a half days long. Diwali falls in the Indian month of Kartika (KAHR-ti-kah). In India, the Diwali festival may last for three days or more, but Hindus in the United States and Canada celebrate for only one day.

Weeks before Diwali, families start getting ready. Houses are cleaned from top to bottom. Many believe that Lakshmi, the goddess of good fortune and wealth, travels the land on Diwali looking into every home. If a home is not

Saris come in many beautiful colors.

clean and if clothes are not washed, then Lakshmi will not bring good fortune to the family.

If a family has enough money, they will buy new clothes for everyone. Women and girls may wear traditional dresses called saris (SAH-rees). A sari is made from yards of material wrapped around the woman's body.

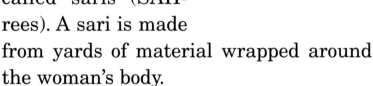

Indian stores sell bolts of beautiful silk and cotton for saris.

Sometimes, the end of the material goes over her head to make a covering. Other times, women wear loose pants with a long tunic-style dress.

Indian stores carry bolts and bolts of silk and cotton material. Indians love color. The brighter and more colorful the better. A sari worn for Diwali is extra fancy. It might have beads

Beautiful clothes and jewelry are an important part of Diwali. So is delicious food!

and sequins, and special stitches with gold thread called embroidery.

On Diwali, some men and boys wear a traditional Indian top called a kurta (KOOR-tah) and loose cotton pants. Others wear their regular clothes.

Gold jewelry is also a part of Diwali. The weeks and days before Diwali are busy times for jewelry stores. Shoppers crowd into the stores. Gold necklaces, earrings, bracelets, and hair clips are displayed. Buyers wait until Diwali to put on their new gold jewelry. On the day of Diwali, they may make an offering of the jewelry to Lakshmi before wearing it.

Diwali is also a holiday of mouthwatering treats. These sweets are given to guests or eaten by family members. It is not unusual to have twelve or more different kinds to serve. Baking all the sweets is a lot of work. Many people prefer to buy desserts rather than make them.

Indian bakeries sell many different kinds of traditional Diwali desserts. Barfi (BAR-fee), made from sugar and milk, is often cut into square or diamond shapes. Laddoos (LA-doos) are sweet yellow balls of candy.

Cham chams (CHAM-chams) are filled with a cheese mixture. Jalebis (JA-le-bees) look like pretzels. They are made from flour, fried in butter, and coated with sugar. Rasgulla (RAS-gu-lah) are cheese balls dipped in sugar syrup. Everything is delicious. It is hard for children to wait for Diwali.

> Indian bakeries sell many different kinds of traditional Diwali desserts. It is hard for children to wait for Diwali.

This woman performs a classic dance at a festival. Around her ankles are rows of tiny bells.

COMMUNITY CELEBRATIONS

DIWALI BRINGS INDIAN FAMILIES TOGETHER. Many times there are events the weekend before or after Diwali. Indian singers and dancers perform. Indian music has its own sound. There are many special instruments like the sitar (si-TAHR), a long-stringed instrument plucked like a guitar; a sarod (SA-rod), an instrument with twenty-five strings; and tablas (TA-blahs), which are drums similar to bongos.

These girls (right) are practicing a dance program for Diwali. Below are traditional Indian instruments. The sitar is played like a guitar. The drum is called a tabla.

Indian dancers wear beautiful costumes. On their ankles they wear rows and rows of tiny bells. As they move, one can hear the tinkling sounds. Many dances tell stories of Hindu gods and heroes. Some men perform special Indian dances.

Some Indians also like to send Diwali cards. The cards have pictures of clay lamps or the goddess Lakshmi. Lakshmi is usually seen seated on the petals of a lotus flower. She wears gold jewelry, and gold coins fall from one of her hands. The words inside the cards wish everyone a year of good fortune.

Sometimes Diwali parties are given for the children by community groups. Children play a game called "pin the flame on the dipa."

It is played just like "pin the tail on the donkey." Instead of a donkey's tail, blindfolded boys and girls have a picture of a flame. They try to stick it on a picture of a dipa, the clay oil lamp.

Indian restaurants are filled with customers eating good Indian food. Indian cooking uses many kinds of spices. There are many kinds of curries. A curry is a dish that has a gravy and is flavored

A group of women attend a Diwali festival in 2004.

with spices. Indians also like to eat rice. Flatbreads made of wheat are eaten with most meals. Pieces of bread are used to pick up the curries and to dip in sauces.

Many different spices are used in Indian food. These were photographed at a market in Delhi, India.

This woman in Agra, India, is making flatbreads.

DIWALI ARRIVES

DIWALI IS CELEBRATED IN MANY DIFFERENT ways. Many Indians will perform a puja in honor of Lakshmi. Some families get up very early, before the sun rises. Quietly, they gather before their home altar and begin their puja ceremony. After the puja, the family eats a big meal with many traditional foods. If Diwali occurs on the weekend, the rest of the day is filled with visiting friends and celebrating.

This rangoli is made of rice flour. Everyone who walks by can see the beautiful peacock.

Some girls spend the day decorating the outside entrance floor of their homes with colored powder. Rice flour is used to make special designs called rangoli (RAN-go-lee). Yellow, red, green, and blue colors are added. The designs of birds and flowers are made by joining together dots. Sometimes girls add words that say, "Welcome" or "Happy Diwali." Everyone

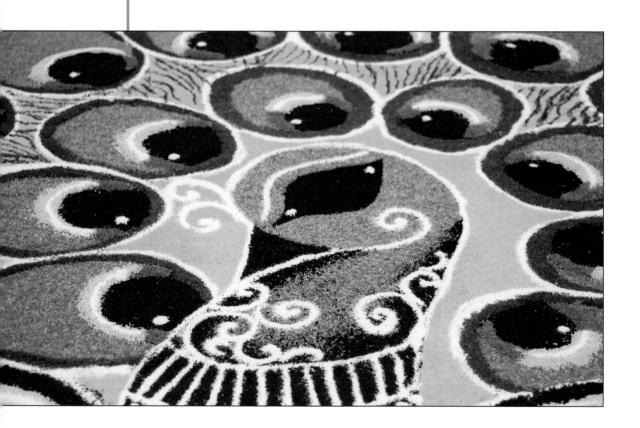

entering the house will walk by the rangoli. The girls hope the beautiful designs will also welcome Lakshmi.

Many shop owners will have two pujas: one at home with their family, and one for their place of business as well. Diwali is very important for business owners. They want the goddess of wealth and good fortune to bless their business. The owners and employees may invite a Hindu

priest to come to their store and perform a puja, asking the goddess to bring them good fortune.

Diwali is the beginning of the new business year. All business books and accounts are closed. Business owners pay any debts. A special symbol is put on the account page to show that one

Indian stock brokers perform a puja to Lakshmi, the goddess of wealth, on Diwali.

Women pray during Diwali at a temple in Los Angeles, California.

business year is ending and a new year is beginning.

Some Hindus attend special Diwali pujas at Hindu temples. After the puja, Hindu priests talk about following the right path to find happiness in this life and in the next.

When Diwali falls during the week, most families in the United States and Canada wait until work and school are over to perform their puja.

When it is time to begin, the family dresses in their new clothes and saris. Everyone removes their shoes in honor of Lakshmi and gathers near the altar. Incense or an oil lamp is lit near a small image of Lakshmi. The father reads from a book and recites the prayers.

An offering of flowers, fruit, and sweets is placed in front of Lakshmi. After the puja, everyone hugs one another.

This person is getting a henna tattoo. These temporary tattoos are worn for special occasions, such as weddings.

43

"Happy Diwali" is repeated to each person. The younger people touch the feet of the grandparents as a sign of respect.

As the sun goes down, it is time to light the small lamps. Some families also use strings of small electric lights. They string the lights along the edges of the roof of their homes. Soon flickering light is everywhere.

> As the lamps burn bright, everyone's wish is that Lakshmi will bring good fortune to all for the coming year.

Now it is time to eat. On the table are plates full of delicious Indian food. After the main meal, the mother brings out a tray filled with sweets and desserts. There is so much food. Family and friends are in a joyous mood.

Indian people love to celebrate Diwali. As the lamps burn bright, the wish of everyone is that Lakshmi will bring good fortune to all for the coming year. Happy Diwali!

WORDS TO KNOW

avatar—A god appearing in human form.

barfi—Candy made from sugar and milk.

Brahma—The Creator; one part of Brahman.

Brahman—The one Supreme Being in Hinduism, who is believed to have three parts.

ceremony—A set of actions done the same way every time, usually to celebrate a special event.

dipa—Small oil lamp made from clay.

exile—To send a person away from their home and country.

jalebis—A Diwali treat shaped like a pretzel.

karma—Actions or deeds.

Krishna—The eighth avatar of Vishnu.

laddoos—Sweet golden-yellow balls of candy.

Lakshmi—The goddess of good fortune and wealth.

puja—A prayer or worship service.

Rama—The seventh avatar of Vishnu.

rangoli—Designs with rice powder that girls put on doorsteps and entrances for Diwali.

rasgulla—Cheese balls dipped in sugar syrup.

reincarnation—The rebirth of a soul as something or someone else.

sari—A garment worn by Indian women. It is made by wrapping yards of material around the body.

Shiva—The Destroyer; one part of Brahman.

sitar—A tall, long-stringed musical instrument played like a guitar.

symbol—Something that stands for a thing or idea.

tablas—Drums that are similar to bongos.

Vedas—Four ancient sacred Hindu writings that have stories about creation, prayers, and the right way to live.

Vishnu—The Preserver; one part of Brahman.

LEARN MORE

Books

Heiligman, Deborah. *Celebrate Diwali*. Washington, D.C.:
   National Geographic, 2006.

Jordan, Denise M. *Diwali*. Chicago, IL: Heinemann
   Library, 2002.

Trueit, Trudi Strain. *Diwali*. New York: Children's Press,
   2006.

Web Sites

Divali (Diwali) for Kids
http://www.woodlands-junior.kent.sch.uk/Homework/
   religion/diwali.htm

Factmonster.com
http://www.factmonster.com/spot/diwali1.html

Kids Web India
http://www.kidswebindia.com/Diwali.php

INDEX